WHITESTONE
OAMARU

A Victorian Architectural Heritage

PETER SHAW

PHOTOGRAPHS BY PETER HALLETT

CRAIG
POTTON
PUBLISHING

WHITESTONE OAMARU
First Published 1995 by
CRAIG POTTON PUBLISHING
PO Box 555, Nelson, New Zealand

Design: Sandipa Gould, One Sky Design
Typesetting & Computer Graphics: Sambodhi Prem
Publishing Coordinator: Robbie Burton
Printed in Hong Kong by Everbest Printing Co Ltd

ISBN 0 908802 30 7

ACKNOWLEDGEMENTS

Many people have been both helpful and encouraging in the research and writing of this book. In particular I would like to thank Bruce McCulloch of the North Otago Museum; Jill Grenfell and Joan Blackburn of Oamaru Public Library; David Polson and Neil Plunket of the Whitestone Civic Trust; Warwick Smith of the Forrester Gallery; Sister Marie Therese of Teschemaker's; Yvonne Walker of the New Zealand Historic Places Trust in Oamaru; Wendy Garvey of the School of Architecture Library, University of Auckland; Clive Lucas, O.B.E. of Clive Lucas, Stapleton and Partners, Sydney.

Once again I am grateful for the availability of a fine thesis from the School of Fine Arts, Christchurch: Connal McCarthy's on the Oamaru architectural practice of Forrester and Lemon.

Coral and Miriam Shaw gave invaluable editorial advice.

Peter Hallett showed patience and tenacity in tracking down the North Otago locations which the text obliged him to seek out. He has of course photographed them all with his customary skill.

I have greatly valued the encouragement of Robbie Burton of Craig Potton Publishing whose involvement in all stages of the book's production has been crucial, as has that of Sandipa Gould of One Sky Design, Nelson who is responsible for its elegant appearance.

Peter Shaw
Auckland
1995

THE SOUTH ISLAND TOWN OF OAMARU, in North Otago, is unique in New Zealand for a number of things, but especially its architecture. Between the years 1870 and 1880 the town experienced a commercial boom which led to the construction of many fine buildings in the region's distinctive creamy white granular limestone now known as Oamaru stone. These durable buildings stand today as a reminder of a vibrant early history. Fortunately for all New Zealanders their survival is assured as the result of preservation and restoration programmes set up by local organisations. It is important that the story of Oamaru be told so that visitors as well as those who live there can fully appreciate a unique Victorian architectural heritage.

It is difficult to be certain about Oamaru's pre-European origins. Early accounts written by Pakeha settlers eager to emphasise their pioneering zeal described the area in tones of boundless confidence. In their view pre-European Oamaru was either wholly deserted by Maori or inhabited by small settlements at the mouths of the rivers Waitaki and Awamoko, and at Moeraki. W.H.S. Roberts, writing in 1906, describes the whole of North Otago as "excellent pastureland, useless to the Maori, patiently waiting for the plucky pioneers to come and stock it."

Roberts had already written in the Canterbury Times of 29 April 1897 that until 1853 Oamaru "was in a state of primeval wilderness, where brown tussock, flax, speargrass and tumatakuru reigned supreme." He noted that Cook had sailed straight past the site of present day Oamaru in February 1770 and that Bishop Selwyn camped one night on the beach there on his way north from Otakou. Such emphasis on the uninhabited nature of the land and its consequent lack of value was frequently pointed out by contemporary historians and commentators whose European notions of land worth accorded with the settlers' own justification for their massive acquisitions.

K.C. McDonald, writing in 1962, comments that it is probable that the Maori population was never large. There is evidence of moa hunters' camps at certain points on the coast but when the huge bird became extinct after AD 1500 the bush-less land apparently had little to offer Maori. As kumara could not be grown so far south people survived by hunting and fishing, only rarely establishing even semi-permanent settlements. There is also evidence of tracks in the area used by traders with northern tribes. As a result of this nomadic way of life most geographical features were named.

The present day tribe most closely associated with the Oamaru area is Ngai Tahu who came from the east coast of the North Island probably at the beginning of the eighteenth century. They were preceded in the late sixteenth century by the Ngati-Mamoe, who executed rock drawings in red ochre or haematite on the walls of caves in which they sheltered while travelling between the coast and their inland villages. These drawings at Takiroa, near Duntroon, are regarded as unusual in being drawn not as individual pictures but as a continuous frieze which unfolds across the lower section of a limestone bluff overlooking the Waitaki River near the township.

At Maerewhenua, North Otago, can be found striking black drawings including a figure given an individual character by its spiral decoration. This may well be older than the Takiroa frieze and is believed to have been executed by an earlier tribe, the Waitaha, who depicted birds, fish and reptiles they encountered on their journey to the district. Later drawings in charcoal at this site depict what seem to be European sailing ships but in fact it is difficult to be certain if the apparent subject of any rock drawing is what the original artists intended to portray.

On 27 December 1836 the Sydney-born whaler John Hughes arrived at Moeraki where he set up the whaling station called Onekaraka with five Europeans and six Maori employees. The place was already occupied by the chief Tangatahara who left shortly after the arrival of the whalers. During 1838 canoes arrived bearing Maori in retreat from Te Rauparaha's northern aggression. They settled nearby, establishing friendly relations with the whalers, some of whom, including Hughes, took wives from their number.

In 1840 Bishop Pompallier visited and in 1842 James Watkin, a Methodist missionary stationed at Waikouaiti, followed. The latter's influence on Moeraki's Maori population was significant, but appalled by stories of their licentious way of life, he ignored the whalers altogether. On 30 July 1843 he baptised the chiefs Matiaha Tiramorehu and Rawiri Te Maramu.

The first European to describe what is now Oamaru was Edward Shortland, who held the Government position of Sub-protector of Aborigines and who had gone to Otago as an interpreter with a commission investigating pre-Treaty of Waitangi

Oamaru and the lower Waitaki basin

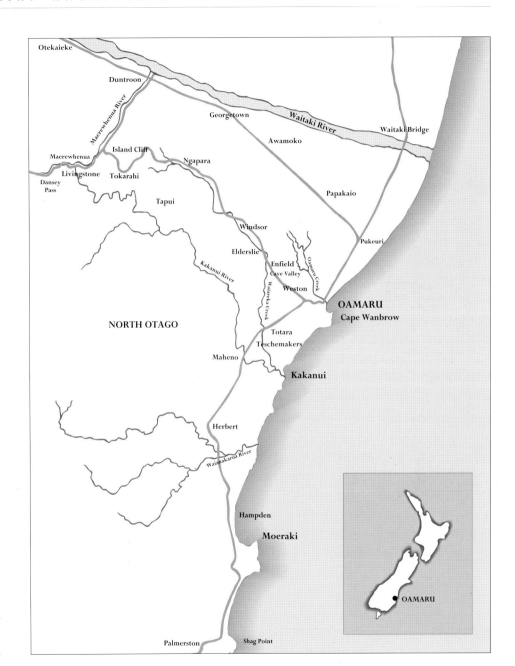

land claims. He took advantage of time spent at Moeraki to explore the surrounding country and on 9 January 1844 stood on a ridge at Cape Wanbrow (Makotukutuku) overlooking the plain on which the town now stands. He went down with his Maori companions to the banks of the Oamaru creek where they had lunch and shot two ducks and two gulls.

In 1848 North Otago passed from Maori into European ownership and European occupation of North Otago thereafter occurred as a matter of course. On 12 June 1848 the Government agent, Tacy Kemp, instigated the purchase of a huge block of land extending from Kaiapoi south to the Otago Block for a cash payment of £2000. It is this tiny sum and the subsequent failure to provide promised benefits to Maori, including guaranteed land reserves, which today form part of the the basis for the Ngai Tahu claim for compensation to the Waitangi Tribunal.

In 1851 rural land became available for settlement in blocks of not more than 640 acres at a price of £1 per acre. Much larger pastoral runs were also made available on a licence-to-occupy basis at a fee of £5 a year. There was a charge of an extra pound for every one thousand sheep over five thousand, the total limit being 25,000 sheep. If a piece of licensed land was required for sale the licence could be terminated at any time, although the run-holder could exercise a pre-emptive right to purchase 80 acres for his homestead.

During 1851 some of the numbered runs were taken up, No. 9 going to John Hughes the whaler, and No's 12 and 13 to the Swede Charles Suisted who in 1848, without legal tenure, had set himself up running

Oamaru from Pukeuri Hill 1872. A watercolour by George O'Brien, Forrester Gallery, Oamaru. Cape Wanbrow is in the middle distance and the future town of Oamaru at the end of the road. *Forrester Gallery.*

sheep at Otepopo near Waianakarua, south of Oamaru. In 1852 new regulations halved the price per acre encouraging the purchase of 80-acre holdings, two of which were purchased by John Lemon, later the partner of Thomas Forrester in what was to become Oamaru's premier architectural practice. A wave of pastoral settlements occured between 1853 and 1856, among them land sold to E.B. Atkinson at Clifton Falls; J.P. Taylor who on-sold to W.H. Dansey at Otekaieke; W.H. Teschemaker and Mark Noble at Kauru – to name but a few of those responsible for erecting noted homesteads in the future.

The first European resident on the site of Oamaru was Hugh Robison who, on 28 February 1853, applied for the licence of Run 15, 'Oamara'. His flock of sheep had arrived at Dunedin from Sydney in June 1852 on the barque *Louisa* but nothing is known of their journey to Oamaru. On his arrival Robison, assisted by three Maori, put up a tent-shaped hut with a sod chimney at one end and a calico door at the other. It was constructed with materials at hand – cabbage tree stems, flax, raupo and clay. He later built a more substantial dwelling with two rooms, a woolshed nearby and a sheep dip. In 1856, for an unknown reason, he sold out to existing runholder W.H. Valpy who in turn on-sold to members of the Filleul family who held the neighbouring coastal run of Papakaio.

Many of these settlers came from origins which in England would have classed them as gentlefolk. A number of the men had university educations, others were the children of clergymen – all would have found the way of life extremely harsh. Domestic arrangements were seldom satisfactory, indeed it is known that limestone caves were frequently used as shelters in the early days. One remains clearly visible on the property known as Calton Hill, named after Edinburgh's well known landmark, in White Rocks Road, Weston, just outside Oamaru.

Here in 1864 Henry Allan backed his earliest dwelling against a wall of limestone in which he carved out a fireplace and other storage spaces. Other early dwellings were made from sods of earth or clay, though the local stone was gradually used once its properties were recognised.

Oamaru was ideally placed to service the runs since its projecting headland offered some shelter for transport by sea in the period before 1860, only after which wheeled vehicles could travel from Dunedin. A roadstead was established to enable Filleul's and Robison's wool to be taken out to a store-carrying schooner which then sailed back to Dunedin carrying bales. In 1858 the provincial government set up a hoisting derrick to help in getting goods from the beach to the top of the bank near the landing.

In the same year H.C. Hertslet of Moeraki moved to Oamaru with a landing crew of Maori. Under Government contract he took charge of loading and unloading operations, leasing a goods store which the Government had built on the beach. According to the recollections of an 'old resident' printed in the Oamaru Mail in 1884, Hertslet was educated at Westminster School, "could think in Latin and Greek, abuse with as much fluency in French and Maori and give practical lessons in the art of self defence to impertinent clients". His Maori employees apparently revelled in their work running the boats out of the surf up the beach. Gradually Oamaru overtook Moeraki as the preferred landing place and steamships began to call regularly. In late 1860 work began on cutting a road to the landing above the beach.

The Oamaru area was still sparsely populated. Although there were no schools, churches, roads, courts, hotels in 1858 two university graduates opened the town's first stores. Charles Traill began business in a tent and lived in a clay-plastered cabbage tree hut south of the creek close to the future site of St Luke's Church. Later, in 1863, trading as

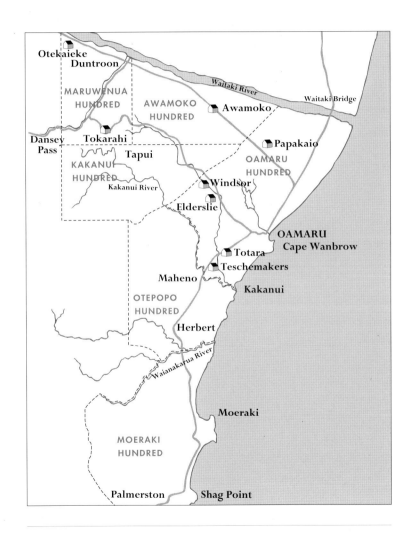

The Hundreds, proclaimed between 1860 and 1865, were designed to break up large run holdings for settlement.

Traill and Roxby, he was to have larger stone premises built to a design of William Mason. Henry France followed after having bought 10 acres of land at Oamaru where he set up as storekeeper, chemist and later postmaster. A doctor too arrived, and purchased land on which to build a house in Humber Street. Hertslet built an accommodation house which is included along with Filleul's station and woolshed, the government store, and Henry France's store in a sketch made on 10 July 1858 by the surveyor John Turnbull Thomson. He also included a site for a bridge over the Oamaru Creek. Later he sent assistant surveyor Edwin Fairburn to carry out a detailed survey which included the streets named after the English and Scottish rivers Thames, Severn, Humber, Dee, Clyde, Tay, Tweed, Tyne, Coquet and Nen, many of which had also been used in the recently surveyed town of Invercargill.

Although there was some consolation in a steady wool price for runholders, tenure remained uncertain particularly after 1860 when the Provincial Government opened up land for smaller settlements by proclaming the "hundreds". Traditionally a hundred was an area of land capable of supporting a hundred people but in fact no limit was imposed on the size of these holdings. They were specifically designed to be taken up by small farmers for 10 shillings an acre (£1 after 1860) and were, on the face of it, a considerable threat to the run holders, many of whom had poured large amounts of capital into their licensed land. With only their pre-emptive right to a smaller purchase available as a means of recouping some of their losses the outlook was apparently far from good. But as ever when land is sold at auction, those with capital were the beneficiaries of the system. There was little effort to prevent the creation of large land holdings by runholders such as McMaster of Tokarahi, Campbell of Otekaieke, Fenwick of Kuriheka, Menlove of Windsor and Reid of Elderslie. Eventually numbers of small farmers found themselves excluded from much of the best land. Those who were successful diversified from wool production and, encouraged by good soil and a favourable climate, began to grow wheat. Oats too, in an age of horse power, were profitably grown as were potatoes.

The Oamaru run had been transferred to James Hassell, an Australian squatter, in 1859. When he failed the following year to get pre-emptive rights to the station's buildings on what was now the Oamaru hundred he moved on to other freehold property. By 1862 the land around the now growing town was surrounded by freehold estates.

In the decade 1860-70 Oamaru was to be transformed by the arrival of new settlers. The population grew steadily from 207 at the end of 1861 to 730 by 1864. Following the discovery of gold in the Lindis in 1861 and the opening up for sale of the first block of rural land near the town, the town itself was set for development. At the first sale of land in the Oamaru Survey District demand was keen. Forty applications were made for the whole block of 3260 acres and 29 others for smaller areas. Again, most of the buyers were runholders or speculators rather than small farmers.

One of the runholders, Mark Noble, built a large square Gothic house in limestone which still stands in Alt Street on land he purchased at this sale. Casa Nova, as it is called, is a rather unprepossessing edifice designed by local builders Glass and Grenfell. No doubt its plain unadorned appearance would have been modified by the barge boards which are no longer a feature of the upper storey of its double storeyed facade.

The number of established businesses grew. In the Wansbeck Street area, the main entry to the town from the south, drapers, grocers, an ironmonger, tailor and clothier, all set up in 1863 premises constructed in the wood and iron of so many colonial towns. In this year Shrimski and Moss, drapers, built the first business premises in Oamaru stone which Roberts described as "the first building in the town with any pretension to architectural style". In 1865 the Bank of New Zealand also erected premises in Oamaru stone. Others apparently resisted it, particularly house builders as it cost six pence a foot at the quarry and the same amount a foot in cartage by bullock dray. It is recorded that the first stone used for building was cut from a large stone pillar which stood on a rise south of the Awamoa Creek called the 'White Rock'. Masons at first used a chisel and mallet to cut the stone but gradually as demand increased the saw came into general use and it was realised that the stone's convenience and cheapness made it preferable as a building material to imported timber. Stone was either smoothed and called ashlar stone, or roughened by adzing with a hammer and chisel in which case the correct term is bolstered stone.

Oamaru stone was quickly to become the single most distinctive feature of the fast growing town's unique architecture for the qualities described by W.N. Blair in a paper read before the Otago Institute on 13 July 1875. He pointed out that supplies of the stone were, for all practical purposes, inexhaustible. At the time of writing there were extensive quarries in the Oamaru district producing cut stone which was used for local needs and exported since 1866 to other parts of the colony or to Melbourne. The constituents of the white granular limestone stone Blair described as being almost the same throughout the province and exhibit remarkable uniformity of colour and texture – "not only can large blocks be got of the same tint and consistency, but whole cities might be built in which one stone could not be distinguished from another."

The first stone masons working in Oamaru had been trained in the use of much harder stone in the British Isles. They did not understand the need to lay cut stone on its natural bed, that is having regard to its grain. Much of the rapid weathering of the earliest buildings was due to the fact that stones were often laid upside down thus increasing the likelihood that dirt and water would sit in the stone rather than drain off, particularly in frosty weather. In one other respect early procedures were perhaps faulty. The practice of placing stones one directly next to the other so that two straight edges were aligned also encouraged weathering. Much preferable in terms of durability was the gradually adopted practice of cutting into the side of each stone with a long 'V' shape so that when placed together a diamond shaped 'joggle' joint is formed. This is then filled with a grouting of lime dust, white cement and sand. Gradually it was recognised too that it was a mistake to lay Oamaru stone directly on to the sandy base of reclaimed land. A concrete foundation was essential to prevent the soft stone sucking up dangerous silts.

Despite these early disadvantages the stone's unique properties as a building material were quickly recognised. In 1865 a powerful crane was installed at the Oamaru jetty to enable immense blocks of stone to be lowered easily into surf boats for transport south where Mason and Clayton's Dunedin Post Office, to be known as The Exchange, was under construction.

In 1864 one of the town's most impressive buildings, the new Post Office in Thames Street, was built to a design by architect William Henry Clayton (1823-1877) later New Zealand's first and only holder of the office of Colonial Architect. Since arriving from Tasmania the previous year he had practised in Dunedin with William Mason. Clayton's small, simple Italianate Post Office sits low on the ground, an impression heightened by the deeply overhanging, heavily bracketed eaves line which characterises both the frontage and all four elevations of its arcaded tower. This never achieved the clock faces intended for its circular openings which to this day read as bull's eye windows. It is Oamaru's oldest surviving public building.

Stone masons working on the facade of the Northern Hotel c. 1880.
Below: **A drawing of St Luke's north elevation signed by Thornley and Armson of Oamaru and by Edward Rumsey of Dunedin.**
North Otago Museum.

The following year work began on the first section of what is today Oamaru's most impressive church, the splendidly Gothic St Luke's Anglican church which commands the corner of Tees and Itchen Streets. It was designed by Edward Rumsey (1824-1909) who had emigrated first to Melbourne and then settled in Dunedin and was a former pupil of the eminent English architect Sir Giles Gilbert Scott, designer in 1860 of Christchurch Cathedral. St Luke's was built in three stages starting in 1865 with the rear nave whose construction was supervised by William Armson (1832-1883), a colleague of Rumsey's at the provincial engineer's department, Dunedin. The completion of the nave was achieved in 1876 and the chancel, tower and spire in 1912. Its exterior walls were of Oamaru stone required in such quantities that a stone cutting machine driven by a 6-horse power engine was brought to the town. The stone was lifted on to a bench and guided to the saw which required a supply of water to prevent friction. Although useful in this large scale job, the cutting machine was found to be too expensive to run and so was little used in the future. After cutting, masons on site still used a chisel to shape the stones.

1865 also saw the commencement of building of Mason and Clayton's St Paul's Presbyterian Church. In his biography of Mason John Stacpoole has described how "the Oamaru congregation found their part-built church merely curious, and, unable to visualise its completion, pulled it down and built a new undistinguished structure on its foundations, thus destroying the concept of what might have been one of the more interesting of the Province's early churches." The problem seems to have arisen when it was realised that the walls of the church were only 10 feet high although the nave height was 45 feet from the ground. Undoubtedly they could not see that the transepts, chancel, square tower and spire of the second stage of contruction would give proportion to the rather squat first stage.

In the rural areas close to the fast growing town there were a number of significant developments which reflected local agricultural and farming efforts. In 1866 what today is known as Clark's Flour Mill was built at Maheno for two wealthy settlers, Matthew Holmes and Henry Campbell, who at that time owned the Totara Estate. They grew wheat, producing 60 bushels per acre, oats and carried some 12,400 sheep.

The following year the whole estate and mill passed to the New Zealand and Australia Land Company which had embarked on a policy of buying up and amalgamating land released for sale after the proclamation of the hundreds. Established in 1866 by Glasgow financier James Morton, the company was an association of syndicates which owned land in Australia and New Zealand, owning 27 estates in Otago and Southland alone. In 1869 they leased the Maheno mill to Messrs Anderson and Mowat who operated it successfully for the next 11 years using the traditional milling technology involving water-powered grinding stones. The site of the mill was unusual in that it was not beside a river. Instead a race was constructed across a bend in the Kakanui river and the mill built beside an outcrop of Oamaru stone which supplied its fabric. Two small stone cottages built nearby provided accommodation for millers.

At Totara itself in 1868 the Land Company built a fine two-storeyed stone residence on a rise near the farm buildings. Its walls are quoined and its roof has a projecting cornice with modillions, an angled bay window and another bow-fronted window with curved glazing. The east elevation has a band of five round-headed windows which form an attractive grouping. Inside there is an arcaded hall defined by two Ionic columns and a cornice with dentils. Elaborate cornices in the elegantly proportioned sitting and dining rooms are testimony to the plasterer's skill and the expense the company was prepared to go to.

The estate was profitably farmed by a number of later owners and after 1880 was the centre of the highly innovative frozen meat exporting trade which had its origins at Totara in 1882. Today the site has been restored by the New Zealand Historic Places Trust and the men's quarters, stables, granary, slaughterhouse site and carcass shed – all constructed in Oamaru stone – can be visited.

Of the year 1867 Roberts wrote that no township in Otago province had made so steady and so satisfactory an advance during the previous six years, having even eclipsed Dunedin itself in the number and importance of buildings erected. It was all the more surprising then that the decade 1870-1880 which witnessed Oamaru's most spectacular architectural developments actually began with a brief commercial depression. Many local merchants ceased operation and the building craze came to a close. The value of property had so declined as the result of over-trading and over-building that it must have appeared at least until 1873 as if progress had simply stopped. Certainly no one could have foreseen that within a short time the centre of the town would have shifted from the Tyne and Itchen Street intersection to Thames Street and that Oamaru would be able to be described as the best built and most mortgaged town in Australasia.

Among those affected by temporary economic setbacks were a number of wealthy landowners whose ties with the district were long established. Although bank foreclosure caused E.B. Atkinson to lose Run No.22 which he had taken up in 1856 and named Clifton Falls, in 1871 he was able to build "The Gorge" at Weston. This fine two-storeyed stone home has been restored and is still surrounded by verandahs on three sides. Two others, John Reid of Elderslie and Robert Campbell of Otekaieke near Duntroon were untouched by the depression and built spectacular houses in the early 1870s.

Reid's 21-roomed mansion called Elderslie, after the estate he had purchased and named in 1865, survived an earthquake in 1880 but not a massive fire in 1957. It was built in 1873 preceded by two years work spent laying out extensive lawns, a sunken rose garden and parterres of flower gardens. 50 acres of English trees and orchards were also planted, the whole scheme being carried out according to a plan said to have been supplied by the great English landscape gardener, Sir Joseph Paxton. Six years after the house was completed Reid planted another 50 acres of Californian redwood trees and diverted the Waiareka Stream through a series of weirs and lakes. The house itself was built in Oamaru stone with extensive iron trellis verandahs. After the 1880 earthquake extensions were carried out in kauri "bricks" which were painted to look like stone. Today only the Elderslie stables, formerly equipped with 50 horse boxes, and the Gate House can still be seen, as can the front steps leading up to the house.

Facing Elderslie was Edward Menlove's two-storeyed stone house, Windsor Park, built only slightly more modestly in 1874. Liveried servants were reputed to wait at table in both houses. Menlove's pig sties were even constructed in Oamaru stone giving them permanence at the expense of light and air.

Neither Elderslie nor Windsor Park quite matched the architectural excess indulged in by Robert Campbell at Otekaieke near Duntroon, where from 1876-1879 he erected a huge 30-roomed Scottish Baronial mansion to a design by Nathaniel Wales of Mason and Wales, Dunedin. Builders used stone quarried out of a nearby hillside from which a special trolley line had been built.

Otekaieke, or Campbell Park, as it has sometimes been known since, was sold to Robert Campbell in 1865 by William Dansey who in turn had it from Robert Taylor in 1858. Campbell was born one of the Campbells

of Duntroon, Scotland in 1843. He was brought up at his family home, Buscot Park, Berkshire and educated at Eton. He arrived in New Zealand in 1860, quickly setting up a partnership at the Galloway Run in Central Otago with family money earned in New South Wales. In early 1863 he

Elderslie in 1902.
Right: **The gates of Elderslie, now at the entry to Oamaru Gardens.**
North Otago Museum.

acquired the enormous Benmore station, followed in rapid succession by Otekaieke and a number of other large holdings. At the time his house was being built Campbell's Otekaieke holdings alone, on which he ran 300,000 sheep, consisted of 85,000 acres of pastoral lease and 17,000 of freehold land.

In 1866 Campbell entered the House of Representatives as member for Oamaru, resigning in 1869 to honeymoon in England with his wife Emma Hawdon. Despite other political appointments his later career was not outstanding due to frequent absences in England, though his involvement in local affairs was both considerable and noteworthy. His enormous home, like John Reid's Elderslie, was the scene of many important social gatherings but drink increasingly undermined Campbell's effectiveness both in business and politics, eventually bringing about the collapse of his health and early death in 1889 at the age of 46. His wife followed him four months later, leaving a bequest which led to the building of a fine church at Duntroon as well as the vicarage and chapel at Kurow which was to be designed by J.M. Forrester.

Otekaieke's Scottish Baronial manner precisely answered the needs of a wealthy young Victorian gentleman who wished to build in a grand style alluding to his own Scottish ancestry. Large scale Victorian castle-styled houses were a common feature of rural Scotland, their architectural details often copied from R.W. Billings' Baronial and Ecclesiastical Antiquities of Scotland which illustrated most of the country's sixteenth-century castles. It is from such buildings that picturesque details such as the bay windows with crow-stepped gables above and

conical roofed turrets at the side of the front elevation of Otekaieke derive, though a castellated or balustraded *porte-cochère* would have been more authentic than the bow-fronted conservatory-like entry at the front of the house. Viewed from the large expanse of formerly extravagantly landscaped ground below the house, Nathaniel Wales's design, so studied in its front elevational symmetry, echoes the work of Scottish Baronial architect David Bryce with its steps and balconies leading the eye up to the central gable.

Inside the conservatory a magnificent tesselated tiled floor leads straight into a columned entrance hall and then on to a stair well lit from far above by a lantern whose coloured glass panes shed multi-coloured rays of light down on walls decorated with richly ornamented plaster motifs. The suspended staircase, said to have been imported from Scotland, leads up to a gallery and bedrooms on the first floor.

The upper floor accommodated servants, of whom there were said to be 40, and was reached by a single steep narrow stairway.

Despite the depression that began the 1870s the construction of one of Oamaru's most impressive public buildings also went ahead. This was R.A. Lawson's 1871 Bank of Otago (since 1873 the National Bank) which with his 1884 Bank of New South Wales (now the Forrester Gallery) forms the town's best-known pair of buildings.

Scottish-born Robert Lawson (1833-1902) received his architectural training in Perth, Aberdeenshire, and Edinburgh. He emigrated to Australia in the wake of the Victorian gold rushes and by 1861 was practising as an architect in Melbourne. In 1862 he won the competition to design

Dunedin's First Church and in the same year moved his practice to that city. While best known as a church architect in the Gothic Revivalist manner, his Edinburgh origins would have ensured his complete familiarity with that city's many Classical and Renaissance revival buildings. Gothic was always regarded as a wholly inappropriate style for commercial buildings such as banks, whereas Greek, Roman and Italian Renaissance styles were suitable for such secular enterprises. In fact, as Jonathan Mané-Wheoki has pointed out, the ultimate source for Lawson's Bank of Otago is likely to have been David Rhind's 1844-46 Commercial Bank of Scotland, Edinburgh. Both share an Italian Renaissance palazzo style fronted by a pedimented portico with six Corinthian columns. The capitals on the Bank of Otago's columns were the work of Dunedin's eminent stone carver J.L. Godfrey who in 1867 had demonstrated to an interested Sir George Grey on a piece of Oamaru stone being used in the construction of Dunedin Post Office "how easily the stone yielded to the chisel" and the delicacy of work possible.

Lawson's other Oamaru building from this period is the 1867 Star and Garter Hotel in Itchen Street on the site formerly occupied by Hertslet's accommodation house. For this Lawson submitted a prize-winning drawing to a competition organised by the Masonic Hall Committee which was to occupy a part of the building. At first only the east wing was built but by July 1868 the whole complex had been completed. On the ground level facing Itchen Street were eight large arched windows and four doorways separated by rusticated pilasters. A balustrade separated the two floors of which the upper had plain squared windows, five on either side of a central slightly projecting bay with a triangular pediment above it. The parapet, later removed like so many in the interests of public safety, was a balustrade topped with carved stone urns. The elaborately ornamented Star and Garter Hotel was soon

to form a notable precedent when other architects were commissioned to build ever grander hotels in Oamaru in order to counteract the impression that the town was a drunken metropolis. In 1872 an event of far-reaching importance for the architecture of Oamaru took place when the partnership of Thomas Forrester (1838-1907) and John Lemon (1828-1900) was established. It was these two men who, more than any others, were responsible for the existence in present-day Oamaru of so many fine Victorian buildings. They were to become the leading architectural practice of North Otago and until 1890 designed nearly all of the town's major public buildings as well as houses, churches, schools and hospitals. Although, as Connal McCarthy has pointed out, in national terms their importance may be rightly described as secondary to that of such figures as Mountfort, Lawson or Armson, their contribution to the region in which they worked was exceptional.

Like Lawson, Glasgow-born Forrester had trained in Scotland, but as a plasterer, his father's trade. He learned how to ornament the interiors of buildings and how to draw plans and decorative designs, adding to the draughting skills he had already learned at the Glasgow School of Art. Like Lawson in Edinburgh, Forrester would have had daily experience of his city's Greek Revival, neo-classical buildings as well as the ornate Renaissance styles which came into fashion after 1840. Ideal as an expression of wealth and status the fashion for the Italianate manner grew rapidly and was to provide a model when Forrester came to design commercial premises in Oamaru.

Thomas Forrester and his wife Elizabeth Megget emigrated to New

R.A. Lawson's Bank of Otago shortly after completion.
North Otago Museum.

Zealand in 1860 with Forrester's parents. Initially both father and son worked in Dunedin as plasterers and later the son alone as a draughtsman with Mason and Clayton. In 1869, by this time employed by Lawson, he was sent to Oamaru to supervise the construction of the Bank of Otago, settling with his family in the town when this assignment was complete. Armed with a glowing testimonial from Lawson he became first Inspector of Works, then Secretary and later Engineer for the Oamaru Harbour Board.

Fortunately, his association with John Lemon allowed him to pursue his interest in practising as an architect at the same time. Jamaican-born Lemon arrived in New Zealand at the age of 21 in 1849. In 1855, after a foray in the Victorian gold rush, he shifted to Oamaru where with his brother Charles he set up a timber yard. In 1868 he was a partner of his father-in-law George Sumpter, soon to become the town's leading merchant. This partnership was dissolved when Lemon and Forrester set up practice.

It is clear that Lemon, while bringing extensive business contacts and a clear administrative head to the practice, had no architectural skills. Instead he supervised the construction of projects and met clients, discussed specifications and saw to the day to day running of the office. Forrester, in full time employ of the Harbour Board, must have frequently been grateful for his partner's skills.

In 1875 Forrester was to design a highly appropriate seal for Oamaru Harbour Board featuring bags of wheat, bales of wool, a heap of large blocks of Oamaru stone, with a cross-cut saw, an ornamental arch above which was suspended a golden fleece. His architectural practice owed its rapid growth and continuing prosperity above all to clients who had made healthy profits from such commodities and to whose aspirations

Forrester and Lemon quickly proved so adept at giving architectural form.

One of the first of these clients was George Sumpter, Lemon's father-in-law. This man, of whom it was said that "there seemed to be no organisation complete without him, no action in which he did not take part" had arrived in Oamaru in 1862. Establishing himself in business as a grain merchant and land agent, he was also at various times Town Clerk, Mayor, Chairman of the Harbour Board, Member of the Provincial Council and foundation board member and secretary of Waitaki Boys' High School. In 1873 Forrester and Lemon designed a gentleman's residence for him in what was then Sumpter's Gully. His house, called Oakleigh, was designed in a simplified Italian Renaissance style. It has symmetrical elevations with bay windows on either side of a central arched doorway from which now projects a rather unpleasant portico. Decoration is restricted to quoins and restrained mouldings. Inside, rooms are arranged around a central hallway which extends the length of the house to a stairway against the back wall.

Forrester and Lemon's first commercial premises were single-storeyed shops for grocers, jewellers and bakers and other small traders concentrated along the the east side of Thames Street. They often featured windows flanked by composite stone pilasters and were surmounted by a simple cornice perhaps with a balustrade or triangular pediment above. In designing business premises Forrester and Lemon were aware that in order to satisfy clients they must provide both visual interest and express commercial confidence, giving an air of permanence to what was after all a relatively recently established town. The most prominent survivor of the many small shops they designed is Meldrum's Bakery of 1879 in Usk Street.

The Ca Corner della Ca Grande on the Grand Canal, Venice, typical of the richly decorated buildings which provided models for fashionable Italianate styles used in London and Glasgow. Forrester and Lemon cleverly exploited their richly sculpted facades to convey a sense of commercial affluence in Oamaru.
Left: Thomas Forrester's design for the seal of Oamaru Harbour Board.

Victorian architects, faced with this challenge, looked primarily to Italian architecture for inspiration. The fifteenth century Renaissance palazzo above all provided the combination of solidity and ornament needed to express business confidence in London, Melbourne, Dunedin and Oamaru. As the Oamaru Mail expressed it on 4 February 1880: "The time is now past when wooden buildings found favour in the eyes of our businessmen, and in the place of unpretentious and plain-looking buildings that used to do duty for all kinds of businesses, Oamaru is now becoming famous for the large and handsome stone structures which are springing up in every street…" Forrester and Lemon were well aware that it was not necessary to depart from established contemporary architectural guidelines laid down in Victorian Britain. On the contrary, to hark back to the old country in building the new brought about a comforting sense of security.

Often they left the sides of a building plain, only decorating the facade, its elaborateness of 'dress' being determined by the function of the building and the size of the client's purse. This presented no problem in such streets as Harbour or Tyne streets where business premises eventually adjoined one another providing an unbroken sequence of two-storeyed facades recalling not the relative emptiness of the average colonial town but the bustling streets of a European city.

In 1874 sections on the Harbour Board block in Tyne Street were sold, initiating a pattern of building which would almost fill the whole block within four years. Here today may be found Forrester and Lemon's 1877 Criterion Hotel, the 1877 Union Offices (now occupied by a bookbinder) and James Johnston's 1881 Smith's Grain Store later the Oamaru Mail building.

Further down are Forrester and Lemon's 1875 Exchange Chambers for George Sumpter and Harbour Chambers for John Lemon himself. These two buildings were identical in design, relatively plain in treatment, and had rectangular undecorated windows and pilasters.

Similarly, another of Forrester and Lemon's early buildings, the single-storeyed grain store of 1875 for A.H. Maude (now the famous Lane's Emulsion building) is not only almost devoid of ornament but was actually constructed not in Oamaru stone but in roughly worked greystone. However, next door J & T. Meek's grain store of 1875-76 has the competitive edge in being more elaborately treated with round-headed windows on each side of a large arched doorway, a panelled entablature, pierced balustrade and central parapet flanked with volutes. George Sumpter's two-storeyed grain store built two years later is still more elaborate with its rusticated ground floor, round-headed windows decorated with three different types of keystones and Corinthian pilasters flanking the two end bays. Forrester and Lemon were always adept at accommodating the demands of clients determined to outdo their commercial rivals by erecting buildings with ever more extravagantly dressed facades.

Such may have been the case with their 1876 building for the Oamaru Harbour Board, at the top of Harbour Street, though the motivation was perhaps different in that the two year old board had no rival. However,

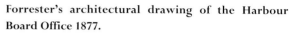

Forrester's architectural drawing of the Harbour Board Office 1877.
Right: **The Criterion Hotel.** *North Otago Museum.*

it was Forrester's own employer. The Harbour Board members comprised the wealthiest members of the community, a group of men poised to spend a huge sum of money on the construction of wharf facilities during the following decade.

The facade of their building displays many decorative flourishes: highly carved consoles supporting a projecting and very prominent cornice; vermiculation of both voussoirs and quoins on the ground floor; composite pilasters, layered one on top of the other; round-headed windows flanked by colonnettes. Forrester alluded quite obviously to Clayton's 1866 Bank of New South Wales in Dunedin; the window treatment on the ground floor of both buildings was nearly identical.

In the case of the three Oamaru hotels designed by Forrester and Lemon the story is also one of progressive elaboration, beginning with the Criterion in 1877 which stands on the corner of Tyne and Harbour Streets. Like many hotels of the time it is situated on a corner site giving direct ground floor access to bar, lounge and dining rooms. The richly detailed facades of the Criterion (now headquarters of the Oamaru Whitestone Civic Trust) are a far cry from the many wooden verandahed hotels in such comparably prosperous northern towns as Thames. The Oamaru Mail commented on 5 September 1881 that "former dilapidated wooden buildings, relics of the early days of the settlement, have one after the other disappeared and in their places have arisen substantial, elegant and commodious edifices, possessing every comfort for the weary traveller."

The 1880 Northern Hotel, like the Criterion, is corner sited, on the intersection of Tyne and Wansbeck Streets. It too has a prominent arched doorway set into an angled bay on the corner and the treatment of the decoration is if anything more elaborate though not as spectacularly so as Queen's Hotel (now the Brydone Hotel) on the corner of Thames and Wear Streets which dates from 1881 but was not completed until the following year. It contained two bars, a large dining room and lounge on the ground floor and 47 bedrooms on the first floor. There are also two stone staircases and a good deal of fine plasterwork inside. The exterior, though similar in composition to the two earlier hotels, was decorated in such a way as to give the illusion of depth to the flat surface by panelling wall surfaces and filling each with pendant ornaments carved in high relief, creating a play of light and shadow. The pilasters themselves are multiples, layered as on the Harbour Board building. Like so many of Oamaru's buildings of this period these three hotels have all lost their balustrading and thus their proper proportions.

Forrester and Lemon also designed many stone villas as residences for clients similar to that in 1879 for Andrew Meldrum next to his bakery in Ure Street, but there were relatively few large residences among their plans and certainly nothing to rival the scale of Elderslie or Otekaieke.

In 1876 they provided the stone mason David Miller with plans for a two storeyed Italianate villa notable for the amount of carved stonework on the pilasters flanking its round-headed windows. The bargeboards too are highly decorated as are the triangular plaster panels at the apex of the gables, something Forrester was to elaborate still further when he

designed the 17-roomed house called Brookfield near Weston for J.C. Gilchrist in 1879. Here all the bay windows have cornices and decorated parapets, while first floor windows are capped with distinctive stone mouldings and medallions under the apex of each gable. A triangular pedimented portico with rusticated Ionic pilasters proclaim a grandly conceived entrance.

Just as Lawson's Star and Garter Hotel had set the model for the provincial grandiosity of Forrester and Lemon's hotels, so too was his 1871 Bank of Otago a pronounced influence on their 1878 Colonial

Bank and 1879 Union Bank of Australia. British precedent had long since determined that the classical style was appropriate for banking insitutions, embodying that essential sense of financial stability and reliability required especially in a growing colonial town. Forrester and Lemon took the notion a step further, preferring to continue with the ornate Renaissance palazzo style instead of utilising the more restrained vocabulary of Greek Revivalism. However, both interior and exterior of the Colonial Bank were restrained in comparison with the Bank of Otago. The ground floor is rusticated with unusually severe

Doric pilasters flanking round-headed windows and a Doric portico. The top floor has Ionic pilasters.

Such was not the case with the Union Bank in Tyne Street which like the Harbour Board office shows Forrester's fondness for the Venetian palazzo which had been much favoured in London, Glasgow and Melbourne. As with the Queen's Hotel the architect concentrated on the use of carved decorative features in high relief so as to maximise a sense of depth, particularly on the ground floor where heavy vermiculated rustication gives a monumental effect contrasting with the delicacy of fluted Corinthian columns and colonnettes which decorate the upper storey.

The junction of Thames, Itchen and Tees Streets forms a unified streetscape like that of Harbour and Tyne Streets. This can be seen from a well known photograph taken by John Megget Forrester at the turn of the century. The 1878 Colonial Bank defines the corner of Itchen Street and the 1885 AMP building the opposite corner, the composition being united by the enormous bulk of Meek's Grain Elevator (1883) at the end of the street. There

is clear evidence here that Forrester and Lemon designed the AMP along the simpler lines of the Colonial Bank in order that the two buildings would relate well together. Their relatively flat facades, lack of sculptural decoration and preference for round headed windows all lend weight to the notion that the architects took some care over this matter. Connal McCarthy comments that "although it is difficult to establish irrevocably that their concern for streetscape was deliberate, there is little doubt that Forrester and Lemon's compact groups of commercial buildings, densely concentrated in key areas of the centre of Oamaru, created a townscape that was unrivalled by any other centre of its size in New Zealand."

Meek's Grain Elevator was a five-storeyed structure 21 metres high, 20 metres wide and 60 metres long with a total floor space of 5,100 square metres. Today it is truncated, having lost its upper two storeys in a fire in 1920, but when it was built its size was

Elevations of Andrew Meldrum house and below, David Miller House.
Left: **The newly completed Queen's Hotel in 1882.** *North Otago Museum.*

23

the admiration of the whole town. As with their other grain stores, Forrester and Lemon only decorated the angled street facades of Meek's Elevator. An elevation of paired round-headed windows ran through to the fourth floor above which a mansard roof with heavily pedimented triangular dormer windows emphasised the unusual height of the building. Wide doors were provided on the ground floor to allow railway trucks to be loaded or unloaded inside the building.

The interior housed 38 large wooden bins, each 6.4 metres deep and in two sizes capable of storing either 1200 or 600 bushels of loose grain. This was kept constantly moving on two elevators which could lift 25 tonnes of grain per hour. 39 metre long leather belts fitted with iron cups revolved perpendicularly around two large worm gears at the top and bottom of the building. The operation was powered by a 10hp water motor, the whole process able to be operated by only five men.

Wheat growing had been at its height during the previous decade when some 400,000 acres were sown, yielding 11 to 13 million sacks per year. Half was exported. In 1874 alone, for example, Edward Menlove at Windsor Park harvested 18,000 sacks and by 1880 the annual tonnage exported from the port of Oamaru had risen to 16,734 tonnes. Meek's Grain Elevator was actually built when the grain industry had already begun to decline. After 1881, when the frozen meat export trade began at Totara, New Zealand's grain export trade declined to the point where the country began to import wheat. Not surprisingly, half of Meek's Elevator's storage bins were eventually removed and the space was used for storing farm requisites instead.

The only other industrial building of comparable size

in the town is New Zealand Loan and Mercantile's store at the end of Harbour Street, which was designed by two surveyors, Dennnison & Grant, in 1882. The most admired and noteworthy features of this building are the architect's decision to refrain from the Renaissance palazzo manner already laid down by Forrester and Lemon and the extraordinary "twisted rope" treatment given window surrounds. Sills on the first floor are unusually deeply grooved to acommodate the need to be able to winch up bags of grain and wool.

Although during the 1880s Forrester and Lemon were ideally placed to get the bulk of the work designing the town's public buildings in Thames Street, other architects were not entirely ignored. In the light of the widespread admiration for his Bank of Otago it is hardly surprising that in 1881 R.A. Lawson was commissioned to design the Bank of New South Wales on the adjoining site. He again designed a Corinthian colonnaded portico to match that of its neighbour but now he enlarged the number of columns from four to six and linked them with balustrading. The new bank, complete by 1883, had no pediment above, the architect instead deciding on a richly decorated entablature above a projecting cornice.

In the same year James Johnston, a former stone mason, designed the altogether more modest Waitaki County Council Chambers (now Community House) in Thames Street distinctly within the Venetian Renaissance palazzo vocabulary of forms. This too has a small Corinthian portico with a triangular pediment flanked on either side by pairs of round-headed windows decorated with vermiculated keystones and Ionic colonnettes and a balustraded pediment. The same architect's 1881 Globe Hotel in Thames Street similarly follows

The junction of Thames, Itchen and Tees Streets at the turn of the century showing the Colonial Bank on the left, the AMP building on the right and Meek's Grain Elevator in the distance. *North Otago Museum*
Left: The Union Bank of Australia 1879. *Forrester Gallery*

precedent. His 1881-82 Smith's Grain Store in Tyne Street with its characteristic Venetian arched windows was originally the most ornamented of all the town's grain stores before it passed to the Oamaru Mail in 1906.

By the early 1880s the citizens of Oamaru, immensely proud of their grand hotels and their commercial and industrial buildings, began to agitate for the government to give attention to the woeful state of their public buildings. Clayton's little 1864 Post Office had long proved too small for its purpose, as had the old stone 1863 Courthouse and 1867 Mechanic's Institute. All three looked decidedly shabby by comparison with their near neighbours. In 1880 the Minister of Public Works visited the town and thereafter funds were released.

The first of the new buildings was for the Oamaru Athenaeum and Mechanics' Institute. Called The Athenaeum, its name followed standard Victorian practice in alluding to the temple in Athens devoted to the literary arts and oratory, dedicated to the goddess Athene. Forrester was a member of the committee and waived his fee for the drawings and specifications he produced in July 1881. These exhibit a neo-classical style characterised by the detached Ionic and Corinthian columns supporting a triangular pediment. McCarthy has pointed out that the fashion for classical pedimented porticos increasingly employed for Oamaru's public buildings ultimately derives from Colen Campbell's 1715 design for Whitehall Palace, London which, like all English Palladian architecture in turn alludes to Greek classical architecture. Such an explicit classical connection in a building devoted to learning and culture or to civic functions reinforced the notion of classical authority so dearly prized in Victorian England. Just as Forrester and Lemon realised the appropriateness of the Renaissance palazzo for hotels and commercial buildings, so too as men very much of their time they knew

when to employ a restrained, more obviously classical style.

The Oamaru Courthouse, decribed in the North Otago Times as "dark, small and inconvenient…a disgrace to the town" was the next candidate for replacement. Here Forrester and Lemon designed what is undoubtedly their finest building. Like P.F.M. Burrows' 1879 Waimate Courthouse, which Forrester would have often seen under construction while supervising the building of his own now demolished Waimate County Council Chambers, the symmetrically conceived Oamaru Courthouse has a central triangular pedimented portico with identical single-storeyed flanking wings. Such a facade expresses the structure of the interior which consists of a tall central courtroom with adjoining offices and corridors. The masses of the building are gradually projected outwards towards the recessed temple-fronted portico. Here Forrester used decoration with restraint, rusticating only the portico's three central entry door surrounds and using carved voluted keystones only on its windows. The keystones of the arched windows on the rest of the building are undecorated. With a reputation for being the best crime producing district in Otago it was perhaps well that Oamaru's new Courthouse should exhibit such restraint to all who beheld it.

The Town Hall and Concert Chamber went to Forrester and Lemon as a matter of course, George Sumpter being the chairman of the Public Hall Company. It has not survived on the corner of Thames and Coquet Streets having been destroyed by fire in 1920. However, the Thames Street elevation was given very plain treatment in no way bearing comparison with either the Courthouse or the Athenaeum. Similarly pared back was the 1884 Customs House (North Otago Arts Society) on the corner of Tyne and Wansbeck Streets with its centrally placed Tuscan portico, soberly conceived in line with current design practice for customs

The Athenaeum, completed in 1882.
North Otago Museum.

The Post Office in Thames Street designed in 1883 is another matter altogether. It relates closely to James Barnet's 1866-74 Sydney Post Office which with its pedimented end bays and central tower were to form a standard throughout Australasia for large Post Offices. Oamaru's is also closely related in this way to Clayton and Burroughs' 1876 Christchurch Post Office and also to Thomas Turnbull's in Wellington, being at the same time.

At Oamaru there were no holds barred in the matter of decoration, though the tower as built is not to Forrester and Lemon's original scheme. This was added ten years later by John Megget Forrester and exhibits some French references, particularly the Flemish mansard roof below which a four-faced clock is framed by a triangular pediment and pilasters. In the original design the tower was to have been square, adorned with pilasters and capped with a cornice surmounted by a cupola. The rusticated ground floor has round-headed windows and arcaded door openings while on the first floor windows are grouped behind a colonnade of engaged Corinthian columns. The two concluding bays, or pavilions, have aedicules (semi-circular pediments) rather than triangular ones.

Connal McCarthy makes interesting observations about the building's French derivations, commenting that its aedicules and ground floor treatment of colonnades and arcades recalls Charles Garnier's admittedly much more elaborate Paris Opera, completed ten years earlier. The grandiose Second Empire style was to become increasingly popular in New Zealand as can be seen in the Auckland Customhouse designed by Thomas Mahoney in 1888 and in Melbourne architects Grainger and d'Ebro's Auckland Public Library of 1887, now Auckland City Art Gallery.

Forrester and Lemon's Oamaru public buildings also included schools, the most important of which is Waitaki Boys' High School designed in 1883. It was preceded by two much smaller schools in the Gothic manner; the 1874 North School in Reed Street and the 1875 one-roomed Maheno school. In 1875 they designed the Grammar School in Severn Street in a plain style except for quoins and a keystone and cornice distinguishing the central doorway from its unornamented wings.

In 1879 Forrester and Lemon became involved with a scheme promoted a year previously by George Sumpter, the Polish-Jewish merchant Samuel Shrimski, and Sir Henry Millar to establish a high school along the lines of an English public school. Forrester designed first the school's seal (its Hebrew inscription probably reflecting Shrimki's influence) and in 1881 won the competition to design the school's buildings, even though his entry had paid no attention at all to the financial constraints imposed by the board. In the face of vocal opposition from the poor, who regarded it as a symbol of privilege, and from Presbyterian clergy to the notion of a school operating in the area as "a radiant centre of culture to the youth of certain classes" building of Waitaki High School went ahead.

Forrester and Lemon's design, often wrongly described as "Elizabethan", in fact most resembles early Victorian English Tudor-Gothic country houses which were much published in architectural magazines of the time. Such houses exhibited Jacobean features such as heavily mullioned bay windows with castellation and steep gables above. Prominent chimney stacks on the original Waitaki buildings, since removed, were another essential element of the style. Waitaki's Oamaru stone facades were enlivened by laying bolstered and ashlar stone in patterns and by decorating gables with drip stones as well as small pilasters in the centre of paired windows. Although the English Tudor-Gothic style had already been used for school buildings in Australia, most notably by William Archer for his 1847 Hutchins School, Hobart, the Waitaki Master's residence, long since known as the Rectory, is one of the first New Zealand examples. As A.R. Tyrell relates, the new school opened, "a fine building placed incongruously on a bleak windswept landscape" with a roll of 19 dayboys on 15 May 1883. The central block followed in 1905 and in 1912 a new classroom block was added at the south end thus forming the group of harmoniously blended buildings conceived by the original architects.

Church design plays only a minor part in Forrester and Lemon's public buildings. In 1873 when it was decided to build a new Presbyterian church it was specifically laid down that its walls were to be at least 7 metres in height, so as to avoid any repetition of the problems caused by the low walls of Mason and Clayton's 1865 original. It appears that Forrester looked at England's great Salisbury Cathedral when detailing St Paul's although it would have been an easy matter simply to copy details of arcaded lancet windows and of the front porch from the many illustrated books on the subject. The style of the church conforms to English Gothic revival practice except that as a Presbyterian church its plan owes more to Lawson's First Church, Dunedin where a cruciform plan was adapted to ensure that 600 or more worshippers could face the centrally positioned pulpit. The decorative carving by David Miller, for whom Forrester and Lemon had already designed a house, is more exuberant than on the more "correct" St Luke's; the absence of the originally designed tower in favour of a belfry and spire and the front porch are evidence of Forrester's free interpretation of Gothic style.

For their next church, St Columba's on the corners of Ure and Wansbeck Streets, Forrester and Lemon changed styles completely. Designed in 1881 and completed by 1883 in a plain classical manner

Thames Street elevation of the Post Office with its tower as originally designed by Thomas Forrester. *North Otago Museum.*

which had no precedent in the town though was popular in Scotland where the rectangular plan provided the simple "preaching box" required by Presbyterian worship. Glasgow had many examples of such churches, the finest of them being those by Alexander "Greek" Thompson built in the 1850s. Columba has an attached Doric portico with square columns at each end, its only conspicous elegance; the interior of the church is unadorned. Its chief feature is its monumentality.

The later 1880s saw the building of some impressive houses both in the town and in the surrounding rural area. Cumbria, designed by an unknown architect, was built in 1885 for Frederick Collis who shortly after his arrival in the town in 1861 had taken up the lease of Hertslet's accommodation house. A two-storeyed villa with bay windows on its ground floor, Cumbria has prominent quoins but little additional ornament. The house was built from Oamaru stone blocks which were transported on drays by two horses from the Fortification Quarry.

In 1884 Forrester and Lemon were responsible for some fine additions to Tokarahi, a house owned by Alex. McMaster. In 1878 he had taken up the homestead property after dissolution of a large holding involving most of the land between Maerewhenua and Awamoko which had been held in partnership since1861 between McMaster and John Borton. The architects' additions to McMaster's 1878 house were designed as a wedding present for their client's wife and involved verandahs at the front of the house and the building of a magnificent double columned and arcaded hall. Forrester and Lemon were also responsible for a granary and cookhouse built of limestone found on the property.

The other notable rural structure from the late 1880s is the stables built at Kuriheka in 1889 by Lieutenant-Colonel J.C. Nicols who in 1885 had bought the Kuriheka Station, near Maheno. The unusual German Gothic design for the stables is said to have been based on plans brought back from Dresden by Colonel Nichols' mother who during 1880-82 had lived in the city. The final design was by engineer/architect T.C. Dennison of Oamaru who retained both the pointed Gothic windows with simple hood mouldings and the ornamental pediment above the door to the upper storey. It is said that Col. Nichols bought Kuriheka for an advantageous price in 1885 yet derived very little from it in the way of revenue until the slump of the mid 1880s known as the Long Depression had ended.

Certainly Oamaru's building boom which had started so promisingly in 1875 had begun to collapse by 1883 and with it the town's prevailing mood of bouyant confidence. Yet in January 1882 no less than 31 buildings were in the course of erection in the town and well over half of the tenders during the three years from 1880 to the end of 1882 had gone to Forrester and Lemon. Between 1885 and 1890 Forrester and Lemon completed only nine buildings compared with more than 40 in the previous nine years. Despite this John Megget Forrester, Thomas's son, joined the firm in 1884 after a period in the building trade. In 1890 the practice of Forrester and Lemon came to an end with the death of John Lemon on 7 May at the age of 62. The final bank statement issued on 22 August 1890 showed only £14 remaining in the account.

One of the practice's last jobs was the design of a huge wooden house for Oamaru's wealthy draper John Bulleid. Although they had already designed his business premises in stone, Forrester and Lemon were obviously intrigued at the client's wish to build an 860 sq metre wooden villa in the latest fashionable manner.

Pen'y'bryn, as the house was called, was designed in 1889. Its Tudor Revival character derives from the half timbering of walls and eaves, the many gables, tall windows and narrow brick chimneys. Such houses, though usually on a smaller scale, rapidly caught on in New Zealand, becoming almost a house style for the architect C.T. Natusch in the lower North Island. It is likely too that John Megget Forrester had some influence in the design of Pen'y'bryn and that he would have relished the opportunity to show his hand at something different. The unsigned plans for the house are most probably his work and certainly the interiors are far more elaborately conceived than anything by his predecessors. There are oak and rimu panels in profusion, carved composite pilasters and a magnificent hooded fireplace embellished with Ionic colonettes and volutes, all testifying to John Megget Forrester's enthusiasm for wood carving. A signed painting of the house by J.M. Forrester also clearly attributes the 1889 house as being his architectural work though there can be no doubt that the later Arts and Crafts additions are his.

The similarly extravagantly conceived wooden house called Burnside, situated near Enfield, was built in 1900 for the eldest of John Reid of Elderslie's seven sons, John Forrester Reid. His father, ever the shrewd businessman, made over the land to his son in anticipation of the Liberal Government pursuing its policy of breaking up the large estates. First instigated in 1894 in response to pressure from those disadvantaged by the Long Depression, the policy enjoyed a wide measure of public support and resulted in the Government's purchasing a number of large land holdings in order to offer them preferably to landless applicants. Even in 1900 John Reid still held 33,000 acres, unlike the former owners of the great estates of Totara or Windsor Park who had reduced their holdings much earlier by private sales.

It is said that on returning from overseas, John Reid was horrified to see the size of the house his son had built at Burnside. The 750 square metre octagonally planned house is by an unknown architect though there have been suggestions that a building originally intended for the site was designed in Scotland and possibly adapted later. However that

may be, construction of the present house was supervised by Salmond and Salmond of Dunedin.

At the centre of the house is an octagonal hall from which rooms radiate in all directions. The hall is lit from above and is provided with a large stone fireplace, a vital necessity in the chill North Otago winter. Door surrounds leading into dining, sitting or bedrooms are elaborately pedimented and a band of decorative ornament in pressed zinc forms a cornice line below the windows. Panels surrounding the main door leading from the exterior verandah into the hall display the finest quality stained glass. Outside on the highly ornate wooden verandahs the letter "E" for Elizabeth, J.F. Reid's wife, features prominently. Above, gables are half-timbered and in addition provided with sinuous French cut bargeboards.

In 1903 another highly atypical building for Oamaru was built by St John Mclean Buckley. He had inherited the Redcastle Estate from his uncle, John Mclean who at the first auction of the Oamaru hundred on 9 May 1861 had purchased 1000 acres to the north of the town which he named Redcastle. This was eventually to become only a small portion of the vast Canterbury and North Otago landholdings he held in partnership with his brothers and which in 1880 were individually reapportioned at the toss of a coin when the partnership was dissolved. John Mclean retired to a bungalow he had built at Redcastle, dying there in 1902. The beneficiary of his large fortune, St John Buckley, began building the house Redcastle soon after, opening it in November 1904 with a lavish housewarming.

No doubt determined by his house's name, Buckley decided on red brick rather than Oamaru stone as the material in which he would build. The architect for this large scale Queen Anne revival house was J.A. Burnside (1856-1920) of Dunedin who was obviously unable to prevent his client ordering French Marseilles tiles for the roof instead of using the more authentic terracotta shingles. Like most buildings in the exuberant Queen Anne manner, Redcastle alludes to a great many decorative styles. Its porch is Italianate and its corner tower Gothic, while much of the additional picturesque detailing in Oamaru stone is even more eclectic. A projecting cornice defines the two floor levels; above it a pattern in red and black painted bricks emphasises the effect still further. Classical allusions abound too: the mullions of paired windows are carved Ionic colonettes and an elaborately carved cartouche and acroterion adorn the arched pediment above the entry porch. The interior of the house was no less elaborate. The panelled hall with its coffered ceiling was dominated by an ungainly archway leading to a carved wooden staircase leading up to bedrooms, bathroom and servants' quarters. Entry to a dining room and a large drawing room was made from either side of the long central hall, at the rear of which was a billiard room. Kitchen, scullery and storerooms were found at the rear of the house.

J.M. Forrester continued his father's practice after 1890 although following the death of his long time partner John Lemon in the same year, Thomas Forrester devoted himself less and less to architecture and more to interests he had long since cultivated in geology, art, history, astronomy and photography. J.M. Forrester's first major building was Weston Hall in 1890, designed in a similarly classical manner to his 1893 "prayer box" Presbyterian church at Papakaio.

In 1892 J.M. Forrester designed St Alban's vicarage and chapel at Kurow. Here he used a restrained English Revival style characterised by half-timbered gable tops, bracketed eaves, square bay windows with hipped roofs and cast iron crestings. The front verandah is wooden and decorated with a frieze of turned spindles. Exterior walls in locally quarried Oamaru stone employ a pattern of contrast frequently noted in

J.M. Forrester's later buildings. Walls are bolstered or roughened while quoins, door and chimney surrounds, string courses and chimneys are in smooth ashlar stone. Tall sash windows light both house and chapel which is connected to the house from its entrance foyer. The architect made every attempt to convey visually the fact that the two buildings were to be seen as intimately related, thus both share similar chimneys and interior ceilings of diagonally laid kauri boards. In 1909 another vicarage in an updated version of the same style was built, this time for St Luke's in Oamaru.

J.M. Forrester's largest building was the Oamaru Town Hall and Concert Chamber designed in 1906 and completed in 1907, the year of his father's death. Built in the Edwardian Baroque manner, Forrester's symmetrical composition is closely related to E.R. Wilson's Invercargill Town Hall of 1906. A towering central pediment which dominates the facade has rusticated pilasters repeated on the two end bays; elsewhere decoration is more restrained though hardly deserving the faint praise sometimes given this building. Perhaps the title Opera House led people to expect something more impressive.

In 1927 Forrester's Hall of Memories at Waitaki Boys' High School was opened by the Duke of York, later King George VI. Its militaristic style reflected the desire of the headmaster, Frank Milner, to build an assembly hall for the school which would commemorate those of its old boys who had died in World War I. J.M. Forrester toured the Great Halls of a number of English public schools in order to study the architectural tradition of such buildings and transplant it successfully to Oamaru. The foundation stone was laid by the Governor-General Lord Jellicoe in1923 but the building was stalled for some years apparently due to difficulties in obtaining Oamaru stone fine enough for the purpose. In the event the walls were built not entirely of Oamaru stone as planned but in

rough hewn basalt with the distinctive cream limestone used only for dressings. For three years skilled stone masons and wood carvers worked on the site decorating the many ornate features of this Tudor-Gothic structure, designed by J.M. Forrester to harmonise with the original school buildings designed by his father. Gothic tracery window surrounds and Tudor castellated towers leave the specator in no doubt as to the building's dual function as memorial and assembly hall.

The other noted architect to work in the Oamaru area was F.W. Petre (1847-1918) who in 1890 was engaged by the Otago Diocese to build a large basilica church in the town. Basilicas had become popular for Roman Catholic churches earlier in the century as a way of emphasising the church's Roman connection and thus distinguishing it from the many Gothic Anglican churches. Oamaru's Catholic congregation was largely of Irish descent; the Irish church had traditionally enjoyed close ties with the church in Rome; therefore a church in basilica form was a foregone conclusion. Also, the basilica plan with its wider nave suited the requirements of the Sacred Congregation of Rites that congregations should be seated as near as possible to the altar and to the officiating priest.

Petre designed the imposing St Patrick's Basilica to dominate the vista down Usk Street from its elevated Reed Street site. Today the cathedral-like church looks still unusually substantial for a town of Oamaru's size but in the 1890s Oamaru's commercial status as a major exporting town would have probably justified such expenditure. The church was, however, built in three stages, the nave opening in 1894, the portico and flanking towers in 1898 and the sanctuary and main dome as late as 1918.

The basilica was constructed of ashlar blocks of Oamaru stone over reinforced concrete, the same combination of materials soon to be used for Christchurch's Cathedral of the Blessed Sacrament, Petre's major work. Although the Oamaru basilica's Corinthian portico is undeniably impressive, its effect is compromised by the domed flanking towers which, although traditional, are not sufficiently integrated with the portico. Another larger central dome rests on a drum decorated with Corinthian pilasters. Inside Corinthian colonnades support an entablature above which a clerestory lights the upper portion of the building dramatically. The deeply coffered ceiling is made of pressed zinc, an economical material which in no way compromised the richness of the decorative effect.

Petre was also the Diocese's architect in 1900 for the Dominican Convent and chapel next door to the basilica and again in 1916 for the Chapel of our Lady of the Rosary at Teschemaker's. This school had been run since 1912 by Dominican nuns on the site of the early runholder W.H. Teschemaker's 1863 Kauru Hill homestead on the Taipo Estate. Petre was engaged to incorporate the homestead into the school buildings. His chapel is an elaborate Gothic exercise in Oamaru stone with flying buttresses, an altar in Carrara marble and a highly ornate plaster ceiling.

Oamaru's legacy of historic buildings now dates from a period more than one hundred years distant from the present and it is this fact which

Work in progress on St Patrick's Basilica c.1898 when the flanking towers had been added but the portico was still to come.
Right: **The interior of the F.W. Petre's Chapel of our Lady of the Rosary at Teschemaker's.** *North Otago Museum.*

has encouraged impressive conservation efforts in the town. The New Zealand Historic Places Trust has been involved with the classification of Oamaru's historic buildings since the late 1970s. In 1987 a New Zealand Tourist and Publicity Department grant enabled the commencement of a feasiblity study of the area to determine long term preservation and re-use of buildings. Many of the precinct's former grain stores and warehouses were at the time used for storage or light industry. Others were empty while very few retained their original functions. In 1989 it was recommended that Oamaru's Harbour/Tyne Street area become an historic precinct on the theme of a Victorian town at work as a means of encouraging the restoration of buildings, some of which were showing distinct signs of wear and tear.

The Whitestone Civic Trust, founded in 1988, encouraged by the Oamaru Borough Council inaugurated a fifteen-year plan which will eventually see the whole area entirely restored and working. Already nine important buildings have been purchased, the facades of a number entirely restored and cleaned and buildings re-tenanted. In the future a series of small working museums is planned. Oamaru's carefully preserved architectural heritage is now increasingly and deservedly valued throughout New Zealand.

OAMARU TOWN CENTRE

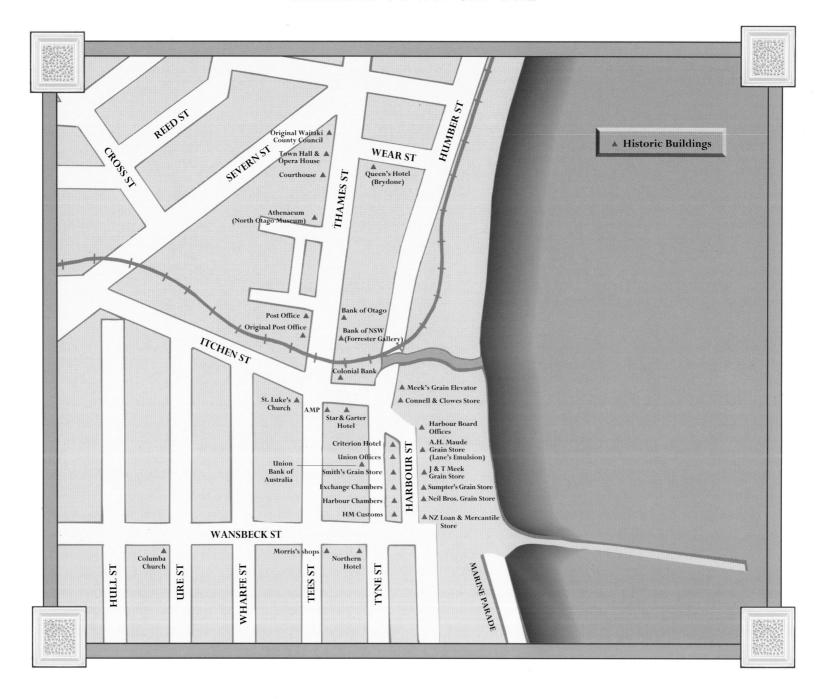

Historic Buildings

REED ST

CROSS ST

SEVERN ST

Original Waitaki
County Council

Town Hall &
Opera House

Courthouse

WEAR ST

HUMBER ST

THAMES ST

Queen's Hotel
(Brydone)

Athenaeum
(North Otago Museum)

Bank of Otago

Post Office

Original Post Office

Bank of NSW
(Forrester Gallery)

ITCHEN ST

Colonial Bank

Meek's Grain Elevator

Connell & Clowes Store

St. Luke's
Church

AMP

Star & Garter
Hotel

Harbour Board
Offices

Criterion Hotel

A.H. Maude
Grain Store
(Lane's Emulsion)

Union Offices

J & T Meek
Grain Store

Union
Bank of
Australia

Smith's Grain Store

Sumpter's Grain Store

HARBOUR ST

Exchange Chambers

Neil Bros. Grain Store

Harbour Chambers

HM Customs

NZ Loan & Mercantile
Store

WANSBECK ST

HULL ST

Columba
Church

URE ST

WHARFE ST

Morris's shops

TEES ST

Northern
Hotel

TYNE ST

MARINE PARADE

For architectural historian John Stacpoole the views down Harbour Street (left) and Tyne Street (right) are "reminiscent of Italy – here if anywhere in New Zealand, Antonio might have bewailed his ship's wreck or Tybalt duelled with Romeo".

Novelist Maurice Shadbolt described the area as having "the haunted atmosphere of an abandoned film set".

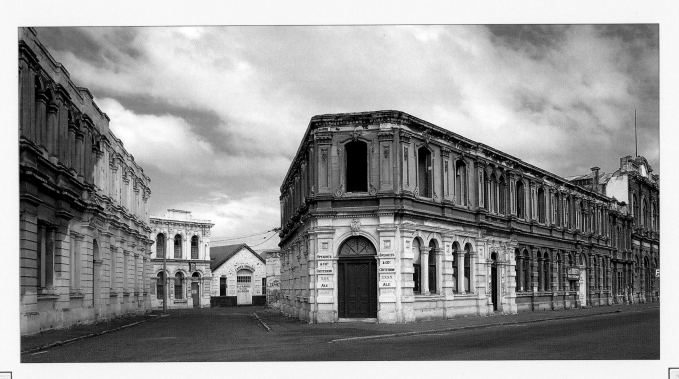

Above: In the late sixteenth century this unusual frieze was drawn in red ochre on limestone by members of the Ngati-Mamoe at Takiroa near the present-day town of Duntroon.

Left: Deeply pitted limestone cliff faces in the Duntroon area provided shelter for nomadic Maori travellers.

Above right: Waianakarua Bridge, opened in 1874, was designed by John Turnbull Thomson, Chief Commisioner of Surveys & Works for Otago Provincial Government.

Right: To direct the flow of storm water, the bases of the Waianakarua Bridge support squinch arches skewed diagonally to the axis of the bridge. Vermiculated, tapered stones define the arches.

Far right: In 1860 this bridge across the Oamaru Creek in Thames Street was built by contractors for the Provincial Government.

Left: Architects Forrester and Lemon designed *Oakleigh* in 1873 for the prominent Oamaru businessman, George Sumpter.

Far left: The Gorge, built in 1872 by early landowner E.B. Atkinson, is a square stone box surrounded by verandahs, designed by Thomas Forrester.

Below: Although John Reid's enormous house called *Elderslie* has not survived, its ruined Gate House which dates from 1873 indicate the scale on which he built.

Right: Vermiculated (worm-tracked) voussoirs define the arches surrounding a door at the Elderslie Gate House.

Far right & below: Much of the interest of the stables at *Elderslie* lies in their many decorative features.

Left: All that remains of Henry Allan's simple dwelling called Calton Hill which was built in 1864 against a limestone wall in the hills above Oamaru.
Below: The early runholder, Mark Noble, built *Casanova*, a Gothic house designed by local builders Glass and Grenfell, in 1861.
Right: Clark's Flour Mill at Maheno was built in 1866 for the New Zealand and Australia Land Co. beside a limestone outcrop which supplied its fabric.
Below right: Flour milling technology utilised intricate joinery in native timbers.

Left: An unknown architect designed the Homestead at Totara in 1868 for the New Zealand and Australia Land Co.

Below left: The Men's Quarters and Cookshop at Totara. Here the New Zealand Historic Places Trust has restored the farm buildings originally built in 1869 by the New Zealand and Australia Land Co. In 1882 they became the centre of New Zealand's first frozen meat shipping activities.

Below & top right: Inside the Men's Quarters.

Below right: The Granary was originally used to store grain but later functioned as a seed cleaning plant and as a venue for harvest balls on the estate.

Below far right: Inside the Totara stables.

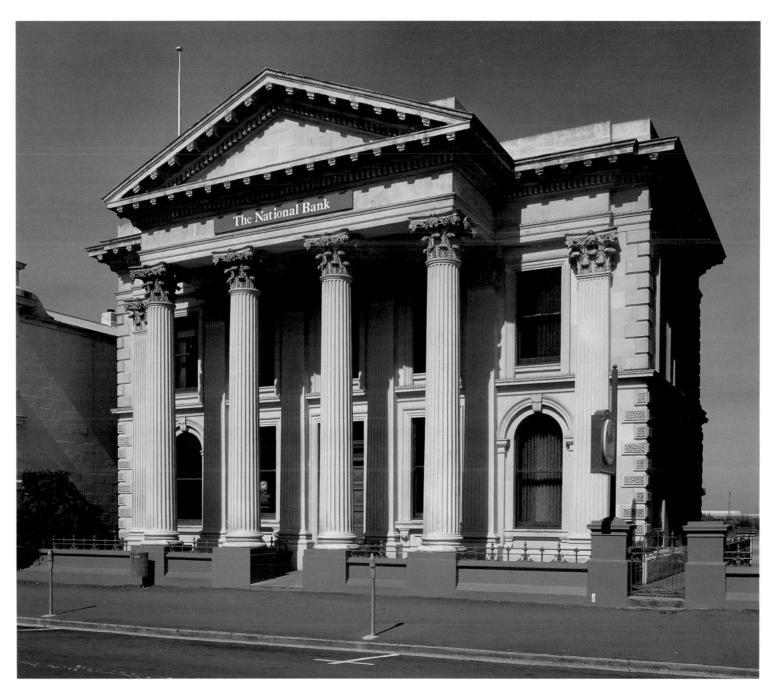

Left: R.A. Lawson's 1871 Bank of Otago, now the National Bank, was designed in the elaborate Italian Renaissance palazzo style considered fashionable for commercial premises in Victorian England and Scotland.

Above: Classical motifs on the triangular tympanum of the Bank of Otago's portico are architecturally correct in every detail.

Above right: One corner of the Bank of Otago's surface elaboration includes a cornice with modillion brackets and rows of dentils, and pilasters crowned with Corinthian capitals and rusticated quoins.

Right: Fluted pilasters supported on bases flank doors and windows on the building's ground floor.

Far right: Carved voluted brackets support a window sill.

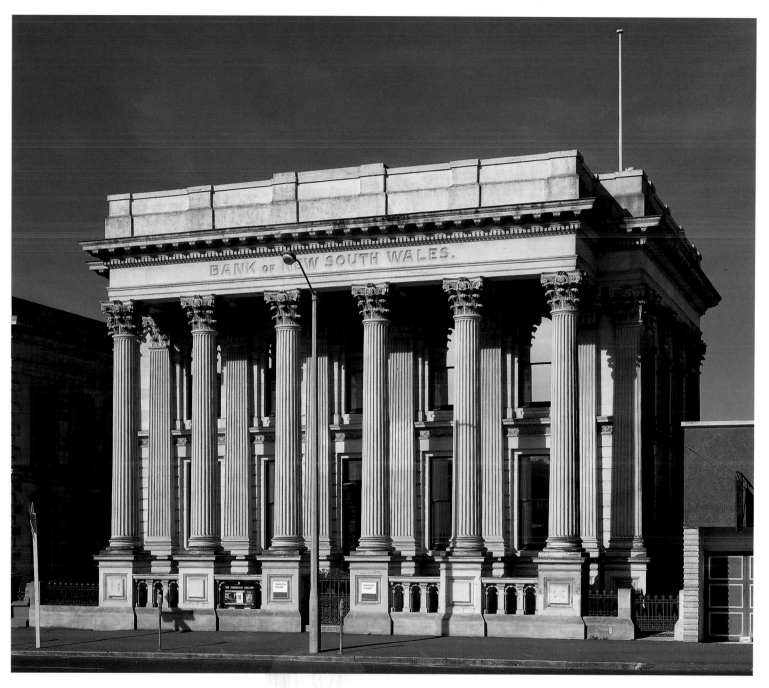

Left: In 1884 R.A. Lawson designed the Bank of New South Wales, now the Forrester Gallery, to be read as a pair with the Bank of Otago next door.
Above: The elaborate plaster ceiling inside the banking chamber.

Far left: The Union Offices during recent cleaning.

Left: Smith's Grain Store designed by James Johnstone in 1881, later the Oamaru Mail building.

Below: The Exchange Chambers built in 1875 for George Sumpter by Forrester and Lemon.

Right: The 1884 Customs Building by Forrester and Lemon is a soberly conceived structure befitting such an institution.

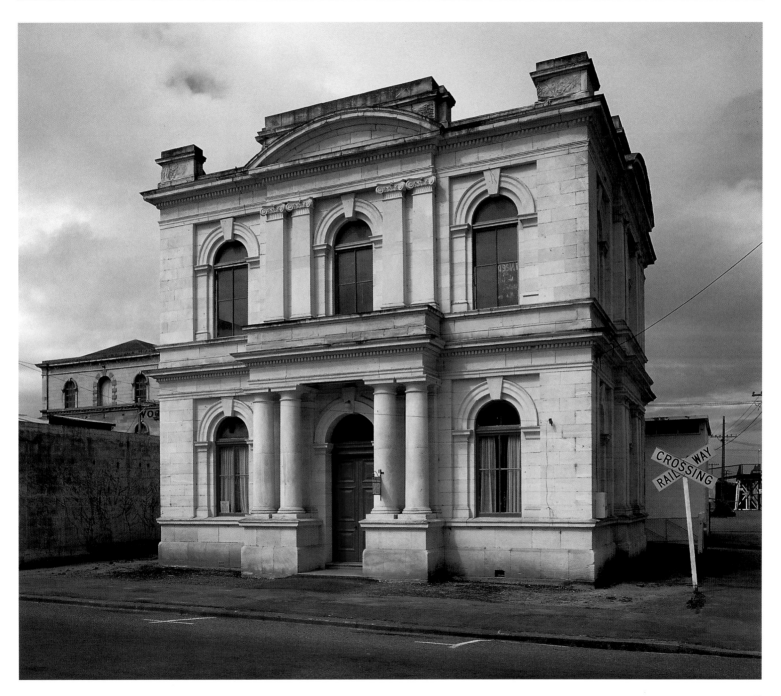

Left: **In Harbour Street Forrester and Lemon designed the Harbour Board building in 1876 using their most elaborate decorative manner to convey a sense of commercial confidence in the town's major enterprise.**

Above: **A.H. Maude's Grain Store, now better known as the Lane's Emulsion building, was designed by Forrester and Lemon in 1875 and built not in Oamaru stone but in a roughly worked local greystone.**

Opposite, clockwise from top left: **Commercial rivals engaged in building new premises tried to outdo each other as the elaborate facade of J.& T. Meek's Grain Store of 1875-76 by Forrester and Lemon shows.**

Sumpter's Grain Store designed by Forrester and Lemon in 1878 has a rusticated ground floor and displays a variety of window treatments.

By the early 1880s wheat growing was declining with the rise of Oamaru's frozen meat shipping industry. Forrester and Lemon's 1882 grain store for Neil Brothers as well as another for Anderson and Mowat reflect the decline in their pared back decoration.

Above left: Forrester and Lemon's AMP building of 1885 was designed in a simpler style in order to convey a visual relationship with their earlier Colonial Bank on the opposite corner.

Far left: In 1879 Forrester and Lemon designed a block of terraced shops for T.Morris in Wansbeck Street.

Left: Forrester and Lemon designed Meek's Grain Elevator in 1883 on the largest scale yet it was only briefly used at its full capacity and lost its two upper storeys in a fire in 1920.

Right: New Zealand Loan and Mercantile Store by surveyor-architects Dennison and Grant, although built as late as 1882, is the town's largest. Its decorative flourishes are noteworthy though sparingly used.

Above left: The facade of the Union Bank of Australia of 1878 by Forrester and Lemon, closely modelled on Venetian Renaissance palazzo architecture, is one of the practice's finest designs.
Far left: Forrester and Lemon's 1882 grain store for T.H. Brown.
Left centre: Meldrum's Bakery designed in 1879 by Forrester and Lemon is a surviving example of one of their smaller shops.
Left: Oamaru's Colonial Bank designed in 1877 by Forrester and Lemon is sadly diminished by the removal of its roof balustrade.
Above: Connell and Clowes Grain Store 1881 by Forrester and Lemon.

Above: The wedged shaped Criterion Hotel of 1877 by Forrester and Lemon is corner sited at the junction of Tyne and Harbour Streets.

Opposite, clockwise from top left: The 1867 Star and Garter Hotel by R.A. Lawson set the standard for the elaborate character of Oamaru's hotels for the next two decades.

The Star and Garter's central bay features a triangular pediment flanked by Lawson's favourite Corinthian pilasters.

Superimposed pilasters at the corners of Queen's Hotel are typical of the decorative high relief on the building's facades.

Forrester and Lemon's 1880 Northern Hotel.

Right: Waitaki County Council Chambers (now Community House) designed in 1881 by James Johnston, a mason turned architect.

Below: A corner detail of the Waitaki County Council Chambers.

Below right: The tympanum of the Waitaki County Council Chambers.

Left: Oamaru Post Office 1884 by Forrester and Lemon with W.H. Clayton's original 1864 Post Office to the left, now restored as the headquarters of the Waitaki District Council.

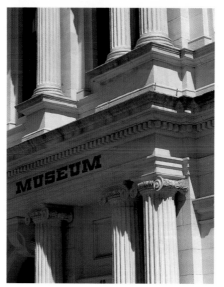

Above: **Oamaru Town Hall and Council Chamber designed by J. M. Forrester.**

Top left: **Athenaeum and Mechanics Institute 1881 by Forrester and Lemon, now North Otago Museum.**

Left: **Ionic capitals decorate columns on the Athenaeum's ground floor.**

Far left: **The Athenaeum's central tympanum.**

Right: **Oamaru Courthouse, designed in 1882-83 by Forrester and Lemon, is generally regarded as the practice's finest building.**

Above: The symmetrical prospect from the former garden at *Otekaieke* 1876-79 by Nathaniel Wales.

Left: The Hall

Far left: The conservatory's tesselated, tiled floor

Above right: The *Otekaieke* stables were built on the grandest scale.

Far right: William Dansey's cottage, built near the cave in 1857 from roughly hewn limestone.

Right: The Gaol at *Otekaieke*.

Far right above: The limestone cave at *Otekaieke* which sheltered J.P. Taylor, an early owner.

Left: Brookfield 1879 by Forrester and Lemon has elaborate gables and an imposing portico.

Below left: Edward Menlove's house, *Windsor Park* was designed in 1874 by an unknown architect.

Below right: Forrester and Lemon designed this elegantly proportioned house in Oamaru for the stone mason David Miller in 1879.

Above right: Pen'y'bryn, a huge wooden villa like Burnside, was designed by J.M. Forrester in 1889.

Right, below: Burnside was designed by an unknown architect and its construction in wood supervised by Salmond and Salmond of Dunedin in 1900.

Far right: Fine stained glass panels in the main door at *Burnside.*

Left: The stone stables at *Kuriheka* were built in 1889 to a German Gothic design.
Above: In 1884 Forrester and Lemon added this beautifully proportioned entrance hall to Alex McMaster's 1878 house at *Tokarahi*.

signed *Cumbria* for the early Oamaru landowner Frederick Collis.

Top: *Redcastle* was built in brick with Oamaru stone facings in 1903 to a design by Dunedin architect J.A.Burnside.

Above: The stables at *Redcastle*.

Right: The porch at *Redcastle*.

Left: **The Central Block at Waitaki Boys' High School was built in 1905.**

Above right: **The South Wing dates from 1912 but was rebuilt in 1921 after a fire the previous year.**

Above: **Thomas Forrester's coat of arms for the school was carved in stone above the Rector's Door.**

Right: **The Rectory at Waitaki Boy's High School designed in 1883 by Forrester and Lemon.**

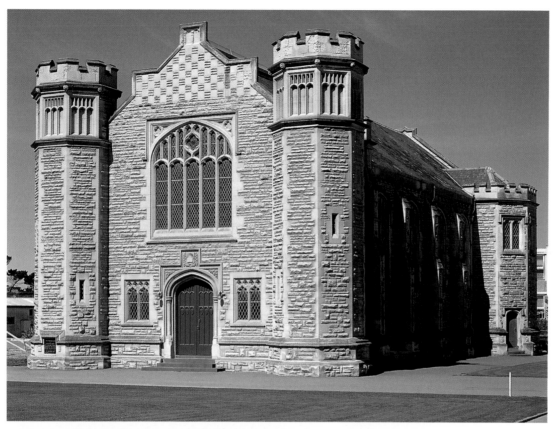

Left: The Hall of Memories at Waitaki Boys' High school was designed by J.M. Forrester in 1923 and opened in 1927 by the Duke of York.

Below, left and right: The Gothic inspired interior of the Hall of Memories is based on similar great halls in English public schools.

Right: St Patrick's Basilica by F.W. Petre was built between 1890 and 1918.

Top left: The Corinthian portico and side towers of St Patrick's Basilica were added in 1898, four years after the nave of the church had opened.

Above: A side elevation of the basilica showing clerestory windows looking towards the rear tower.

Left: Corinthian colonnades dominate the interior which is lit by a clerestory above.

Above right: The Convent chapel.

Above, far right: Petre designed a Convent next door to the basilica in 1900.

Left: The walls of the Chapel of Our Lady of the Rosary at Teschemaker's are supported by Gothic flying buttresses.

Below: The apse of the chapel.

Above: St Luke's Anglican Church, designed by Edward Rumsey in 1865, was completed finally in 1912.

Left: St Paul's Presbyterian Church was designed by Forrester and Lemon in 1873 in a free Gothic style.

Above Right: A porch at St Luke's.

Right: The 1909 vicarage for St Luke's Church, Oamaru by J.M. Forrester.

Left: Columba Presbyterian Church was designed in a plain classical manner in 1881 by Forrester and Lemon.

Right: J.M. Forrester's 1893 "prayer box" Presbyterian Church at Papakaio.

Below and below right: This imposing vicarage and chapel at Kurow were designed in 1892 by J.M. Forrester.

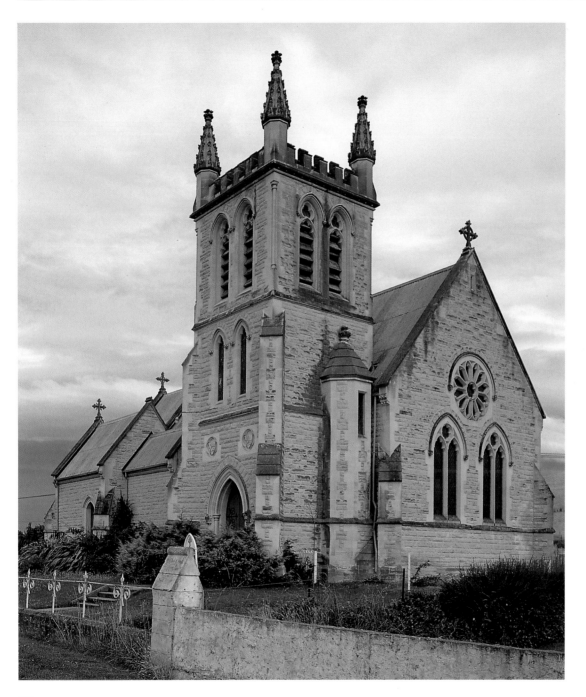

Left: St Martin's Church, Duntroon was built in 1900 with funds provided from the estate of Emma Campbell of *Otekaieke.*

BIBLIOGRAPHY

Brocklebank, Norris and Greenaway, Richard.
Oamaru.
John McIndoe, Dunedin, 1979

Cox, Philip and Lucas, Clive.
Australian Colonial Architecture.
Lansdowne, Sydney, 1978

Galer, Lois.
Houses and Homes.
Allied Press, Dunedin, 1981

McCarthy, P.C.
Victorian Oamaru:
The Architecture of Forrester and Lemon.
University of Canterbury unpublished
M.A. thesis, 1986

McDonald, K.C.
White Stone Country.
North Otago Centennial Committee, Oamaru,
1962.
Reprinted by Capper Press, Christchurch, 1977

Olssen, Erik.
A History of Otago.
John McIndoe, Dunedin, 1987

Porter, Frances (ed.)
Historic Buildings of New Zealand:
South Island.
Methuen, Auckland, 1983

Roberts, W.H.S.
The History of Oamaru and North Otago,
New Zealand, from 1853 to the end of
1889.
Andrew Fraser, Oamaru, 1890

Roberts, W.H.S.
Beginnings; Early History of North Otago
from 1853.
Oamaru Mail, Oamaru, 1978.

Scotter, W.H.
Run, Estate and Farm, A History of the
Kakanui and Waiareka Valleys, North
Otago.
Otago Centennial Historical Publications 1948.
Reprinted by Capper Press, Christchurch, 1978

Shaw, Peter.
New Zealand Architecture from
Polynesian Beginnings to 1990.
Hodder and Stoughton, 1991

Stacpoole, John.
Colonial Architecture in New Zealand.
Reed, 1976

Stacpoole, John.
William Mason,
The First New Zealand Architect.
Oxford/Auckland University Press, 1971

Thornton, G. G.
New Zealand's Industrial Heritage.
Reed, Wellington, 1982

Tyrrell, A.R.
Strong to Endure,
Waitaki Boys' High School 1883-1983.
Waitaki High School Old Boys' Association, 1983

The Dictionary of New Zealand
Biography, Volume Two 1870-1900.
Bridget Williams Books/Department of Internal
Affairs, 1993

The Cyclopaedia of New Zealand,
Volume 4, Otago and Southland.
The Cyclopaedia Co., Christchurch, 1905

GLOSSARY

Acroterion   a scalloped acanthus leaf usually placed on the apex of a pediment.

Aedicule   the framing of a door or window with columns, piers or pilasters supporting an entablature and pediment.

Balustrade   a railing system found along the edge of a balcony or parapet.

Bargeboard   a (frequently decorated) board that hangs from the projecting edge of a roof and hides the horizontal roof timbers.

Basilica   a church divided into a central high nave, lit by a clerestory, with two or more aisles along its sides.

Bracket   a small piece of stone or wood designed to carry a projecting weight (e.g. a cornice).

Buttress   a mass of masonry projecting from or built against a wall to give added strength.

Capital   the decorated head of a column or pilaster.

Cartouche   a carved or painted ornamental panel resembling a sheet of paper with its edges turned over.

Castellation   a form of ornamentation in which a house is given crenellated battlements like those of a fortified castle.

Clerestory   the upper zone of a wall pierced by windows to admit light into a church or room.

Colonnade   a row of columns supporting an entablature, arches or roof.

Colonnette   a small column.

Corinthian order   the slenderest and most ornate of the three Greek orders, characterised by a bell-shaped capital with two rows of sculpted acanthus leaves and an elaborate cornice.

Cornice   a moulded projection crowning a building, wall or arch. In Classical architecture the term refers to the top, projecting section of an entablature.

Cresting   decoration along the ridges of a roof.

Cupola   a domed roof on a circular base, often set on the ridge of a roof.

Dentil   one of a band of small, square, tooth-like blocks that form part of the characteristic ornamentation of cornices on Classical buildings.

Doric order   the plainest and sturdiest of the three orders, the Doric has a fluted column with a simple capital.

Dripstone   a stone moulding that projects over and around the head of a doorway or window and throws off rainwater.

Entablature   In Classical architecture, the elaborate beam carried by columns, and divided horizontally into architrave, frieze and cornice.

Half timbering   a method of construction in which walls have a timber framework with spaces filled with plaster or brick.

Ionic order   a column characterised by a capital with large volutes.

Lantern   a windowed superstructure crowning a roof or dome.

Mansard roof   a roof having two slopes on each face, the lower one very steep, the upper of a low pitch.

Moulding   continuous lines ornamentally grooved (concave) or projected (convex).

Modillion   a horizontal bracket, often in the form of a carved scroll, supporting a cornice or eaves.

Parapet   a low wall at the edge of a roof, battlement or balcony.

Pediment   in Classical architecture, the triangular gable at the end of a roof.

Pilaster   a shallow pier or rectangular column that projects slightly from a wall and may be decorated with one of the Classical orders.

Portico   a roofed space, either open or partially enclosed, which forms the entrance and centre-piece of the facade of a house, temple or church.

Quoin   the external angle of a building or wall, or the large corner stones used to dress the angle.

Rustication   originally the working of external blocks of stone with a hammer to give a rough surface. Can also refer to the laying of blocks of stone with recessed margins, thus accentuating the joins.

Spindle   small turned cylinders, used horizontally in a series for decoration.

Tympanum   the vertical triangular space between the horizontal and raked courses of a pediment.

Vermiculation   an ornamental imitation on stone facings of the tracks made by a wood worm.

Volute   a spiral scroll which forms the distinctive feature of an Ionic capital and can also be used as a bracket.

Voussoir   one of the wedge-shaped stones of an arch.